COOL COMPETITIONS

Astonishing

ROBOT

COMPETITIONS

R. BAKER

raintree 🌱

a Capstone company — publishers for children

Raintree is an imprint of Capstone Global Library Limited,
a company incorporated in England and Wales having its registered office at
264 Banbury Road, Oxford, OX2 7DY – Registered company number: 6695582

www.raintree.co.uk
myorders@raintree.co.uk

Edited by Aaron Sautter
Designed by Kyle Grenz
Picture research by Eric Gohl
Production by Steve Walker
Printed and bound in China

ISBN 978 1 474 74459 1
22 21 20 19 18 17
10 9 8 7 6 5 4 3 2 1

British Library Cataloguing in Publication Data
A full catalogue record for this book is available from the British Library.

Acknowledgements
We would like to thank the following for permission to reproduce photographs:
Alamy: US Navy Photo, 12; Newscom: AFLO/Rodrigo Reyes Marin, 27, picture-alliance/dpa/
Sebastian Willnow, 21, Xinhua News Agency/Li Changxiang, 7, ZUMA Press/Robin Nelson,
8; RoboGames.net: Alan Musselman, 17, Ariel Zambelich, 15, Dave Schumaker, 22–23, 28–29,
R-TEAM Robotics, 24, Sam Coniglio, 5, 18; Shutterstock: phipatbig, cover (right), Roman Sotola,
cover (left); Stefan Hrabar/CSIRO: 11

Every effort has been made to contact copyright holders of material reproduced in this book.
Any omissions will be rectified in subsequent printings if notice is given to the publisher.

0517/CA21700461 042017 4655

CONTENTS ▶

BRING ON THE ROBOTS!

▶ **Robots** are useful in many ways. They can help to clean homes, build cars or grow crops. Some even explore space. But robots can also be a lot of fun. Many people around the world like to show off their robots in competitions.

FACT

The two main types of robot competitions include **autonomous** and tele-operated. Autonomous robots move and take actions on their own. People control tele-operated robots with remote controls.

robot – machine programmed to do jobs usually
   performed by a person

autonomous – able to control oneself; autonomous
   robots are not controlled by a person

AND THE WINNER IS...

▶ People **program** robots to do many things. In skill challenges, competitors build robots to complete tasks quickly and accurately. They then compete to see which robot will win.

program – to enter a series of step-by-step instructions into a computer or robot that tells it what to do

engineer – someone trained to design and build things

Many schools and businesses hold robot competitions. They hope to encourage young people to become scientists and **engineers**.

FIRST competition

The FIRST competition features teams of young robot designers. Teams build robots to solve problems or complete tasks. The robots may need to stack objects or shoot balls at a goal. Teams win by earning the most points.

FACT

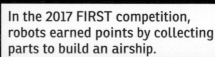

In the 2017 FIRST competition, robots earned points by collecting parts to build an airship.

UAV Challenge-Outback Rescue

The **UAV** Challenge-**Outback** Rescue is held each year in Australia. In this event, teams fly unmanned robotic aircraft. They compete to find a **mannequin** in the wilderness. They also try to drop supplies as close to it as possible.

UAV – unmanned aerial vehicle; a robotic aircraft piloted by remote control

outback – flat desert areas of Australia; few people live in the outback

mannequin – life-sized model of a human

FACT

The winning team of the Outback Rescue
challenge receives a $50,000 (AU) grand prize.

In 2014 the MUROC DareDivas team won first
place in the Airborne Delivery Challenge.

Primary school children can also compete
at RoboSub. They build SeaPerch robots
that explore underwater.

Robosub

Each year in the United States, teams of students take robots under water in the RoboSub contest. The robots earn points by travelling through **obstacles** and firing **torpedoes**. The team with the most points in the finals wins.

obstacle – something that gets in the way or blocks progress

torpedo – underwater missile

US National Robotics Challenge

The US National Robotics Challenge (NRC) is open to secondary school and university students. Contestants can compete in 13 different categories. They build manufacturing robots, rescue robots, combat robots and more.

THE THRILL OF VICTORY

▶ The contestants race, kick, and punch as they compete. But these athletes aren't human – they're robots. They compete with gears, wheels, and metal **limbs**. In the crowd, fans cheer for their favourite robots!

limb – part of the body used in moving or grasping; arms and legs are limbs

FACT

The Robogames has an ArtBot-Musical competition. Robots play instruments, such as pianos or drums, on their own.

Robogames

The Robogames is like the Olympics for robots. Robots may compete in weightlifting, boxing, street hockey and many other events. **Humanoid** robots also compete in football matches.

humanoid – having human form or characteristics; a humanoid robot is shaped somewhat like a human

RoboCup football

Each year, teams from around the world compete in the RoboCup football **tournament**. It includes both rolling and humanoid robots. Rolling robots push a ball around the pitch. Humanoid robots walk, run and kick the ball.

tournament – series of matches between several players or teams, ending with one winner

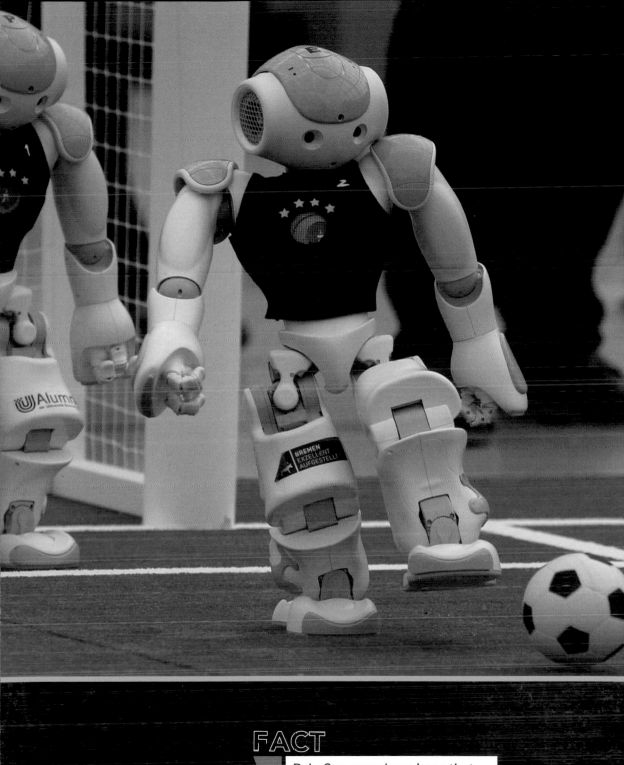

CLASH OF THE BOTS

▶ Smash! Crash! Crunch! Sparks fly during robot battles. Teams create the fastest and toughest robots they can. They build robots with spinning saws, smashing hammers and grasping claws. It's time for a robot rumble!

The first major robot battle took place at the Critter Crunch in 1989. The winning robot defeated the others while spraying a can of Silly String.

Robots in Mech Warfare face off
in miniature models of cities.

Mech Warfare

At the RoboGames, one popular event is Mech Warfare. Robots may have up to six legs. They fight with mini **flame-throwers**, mini rockets and other weapons. The last robot standing wins.

flame-thrower – weapon that shoots a stream of burning liquid

Wrestling bots

In Japan, FujiSoft, Inc. hosts the FSI-All Japan Robot Sumo Tournament each year. The battles are like sumo matches. The robots score points by pushing their opponents out of the ring. The first robot to win two out of three matches wins.

If a sumo robot tips over, it is allowed to right itself if it's still inside the ring.

BattleBots

In BattleBots, arenas are filled with fire, saw blades and floor spikes. Tough robots try to destroy their opponents. They fight for three minutes or until one can't move. Teams keep battling until one is named the champion.

FACT
Losing BattleBot teams have one more chance to show off their robots. During the Robot Rumble, each robot tries to disable as many opponents as possible.

Glossary

autonomous able to control oneself; autonomous robots are not controlled by a person

engineer someone trained to design and build things

flame-thrower weapon that shoots a stream of burning liquid

humanoid having human form or characteristics; a humanoid robot is shaped somewhat like a human

limb part of the body used in moving or grasping; arms and legs are limbs

mannequin life-sized model of a human

obstacle something that gets in the way or blocks progress

outback flat desert areas of Australia; few people live in the outback

program to enter a series of step-by-step instructions into a computer or robot that tells it what to do

robot machine programmed to do jobs usually performed by a person

torpedo underwater missile

tournament series of matches between several players or teams, ending with one winner

UAV unmanned aerial vehicle; a robotic aircraft piloted by remote control

Read more

Arctic Adventure (Robot Races), Axel Lewis
(Curious Fox, 2013)

Everything Robotics: All the Photos, Facts, and Fun!
(National Geographic Kids Everything), Jennifer Swanson
(National Geographic Children's Books, 2016)

Mars Rover Driver (The Coolest Jobs on the Planet),
Scott Maxwell and Catherine Chambers (Raintree, 2014)

Websites

www.dkfindout.com/uk/computer-coding/
Find out more about computer programming and
the languages we use to communicate with robots.

**www.nasa.gov/mission_pages/mars/missions/
index.html**
Find all the latest news about NASA's robotic
space missions.

Index